# K-State: An Alphabet Journey Across Campus

Debbie Mercer and Lotta Larson

Design and Layout by Mary Hammel

Photography by Kansas State University Photography Services, Mary Hammel, Debbie Mercer, and Fred Bradley

Cover Design by Kevin Robel of Robel Graphics

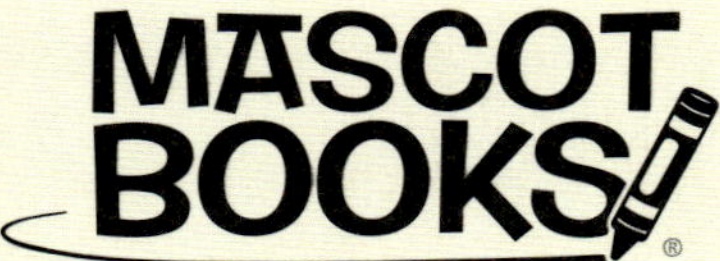


**www.mascotbooks.com**

***K-State: An Alphabet Journey Across Campus***



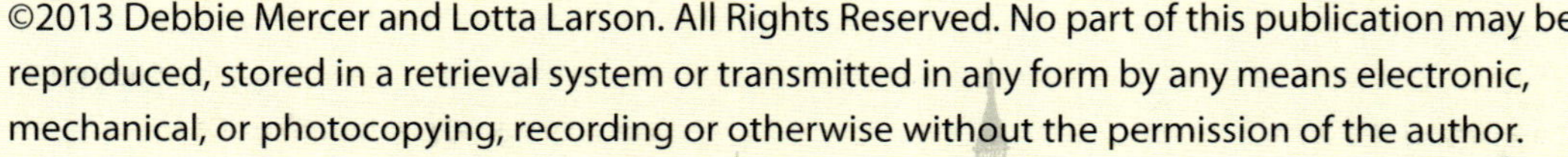

**For more information, please contact:**
Mascot Books
560 Herndon Parkway #120
Herndon, VA 20170
info@mascotbooks.com

CPSIA Code: PRT1213A
ISBN-10: 1620865157
ISBN-13: 9781620865156



Printed in the United States

# Family…

At Kansas State University, family is more than just a word. With eight (not a typo!) K-State degrees between the two of us, we have experienced K-State from the perspectives of undergraduate students, graduate students, and now as faculty and administrator. Each layer has added to our admiration and respect for what it means to be a Wildcat and a member of the K-State family.

We embarked on this book journey because of our love of literature and this university. There were many things to think about as we began contemplating how to create an alphabet book. What should each letter stand for? How could we possibly choose one concept for each letter? After our own initial brainstorming session, we turned to our K-State family for help. Undergraduate students from the Kappa Delta Pi honor society and graduate students in the reading specialist program, both within the College of Education, helped us decide how each letter represents K-State. Countless colleagues and friends in hallways and on sidewalks across campus provided suggestions. Special recognition goes to Dr. Marjorie Hancock, our doctoral advisor and KSU professor emerita. Her love of language, appreciation for children's books, and unwavering support gave us the courage to begin this writing journey.

Many people have contributed to making K-State what it is today. Recognizing the impossible task of acknowledging each contributor, this book identifies landmarks and events that have become permanent parts of the K-State campus. We do not attempt to be inclusive, but to provide a broad range of K-State memories and celebrations. Included on each page are other "letter" words, all worthy of their own couplet.

It is with great appreciation that we recognize our collaborators: Dave Mayes and his staff from K-State's University Photography Services, Fred Bradley, and of course, Mary Hammel. She brought everything together into one cohesive book. In this book the photographs bring the K-State campus to life and illuminate the words in our text. Without their help and support, this alphabet journey would not have come to end.

Finally, we must thank our own families: parents who have always supported our educational endeavors, strong husbands who continue to stand beside us, and our children and grandchildren who offered sparks and spontaneous critiques. Their encouragement and support made the journey possible.

We hope this book brings back memories of your time on the K-State campus… including adventures and academics, friends and family, and games and graduation. We encourage you to share your K-State journey with special people in your own life…those that you call family.

D Mercer    Lotta Larson

Alumni
Ambassadors
Anatomy and Physiology
Aggieville
Ackert Hall  
Alma Mater
Anderson Hall
Agriculture Economics
Aerospace Studies
Army ROTC
Architecture
Admissions

# A

From the academic spire on Anderson Hall
To the athletic fans in Ahearn
**A** begins our K-State journey
As through this book special memories return.

For **B** we head to Bramlage Coliseum
And its popular basketball court,
Where the K-State band plays and students cheer
Providing our 'Cats with great support.

# C

The Collegian's role is to keep us informed
Of events on campus, courts, and fields.
**C** is for celebrating accomplishments
When great KSU news is revealed.

# D

**D** is for dorms where K-State roommates
Live, sleep, and play
Waiting for care packages from home
To brighten their day.

E begins EMAW
The message is clear
Every Man a Wildcat
Willie is the mascot we love here!

# F

Football fans, second to none…proclaiming,
That's good for another Wildcat "first down!"
High five your neighbors, the fun's just begun
**F** is for the sport that lights up our town.

# G

**G** celebrates K-State graduation
And an academic job well done!
With diplomas in hands and caps on their heads,
Students march into the world, one by one.

**H** stands for Hale Library
Where minds grow and bloom.
Around the clock K-State students study
In the "Harry Potter" room.

# I

**I** represents K-State's ice cream
35 flavors made in Call Hall
Fresh from the K-State dairy
Come try them all!

Journalism and Mass Communications

# J

Jardine

**J** houses Jardine Terrace
Students' home away from home.
International students, couples, and families
Bonded for life, wherever they roam.

JP's

Justin Hall

Johnson Center for Basic Cancer Research

# K

Willie and fans proudly spell
With arms and legs…“K….S….U….”
**K** stands for Kansas State University,
You can proudly chant it, too!

Lovers Lane

Limestone

Leasure Hall

Landscape Architecture Regional and Community Planning

# L

L honors our Land Grant College
Established in 1863
Serving the people of Kansas, the nation, and the world
While embracing diversity.

# M

Arriving on the steamboat Hartford
Looking for a place to settle down,
**M** represents the first Manhattan residents
Who established our thriving prairie town.

Nichols Gymnasium

Networks

Number 1 Kansas University!

# N

Never alone

NBAF

**N** stands for never alone…
Students, faculty, and alumni together
All part of the Wildcat family
Creating K-State memories that last forever.

Noise in Bramlage and Snyder stadiums

Nuclear Engineering

Natatorium

Nicknames

Nichol's Fire (Wabash)

# O

**O** is for orientation and Wildcat Warm-up
Where classes are chosen and new friends meet,
By learning K-State history and traditions
Freshmen jitters quickly retreat.

One dollar UPC movies
Orientation and Enrollment
Open House
Octagon of Doom
Olathe Campus
Old buildings
"Once a Wildcat, Always a Wildcat"
Old Stadium

Pride of Wildcat Land Political Science Putnam Hall Physics Purple

Plant Pathology Professors Pedestrians Philosophy Pillsbury Crossing Psychology

# P

**P** stands for purple
The respected color we bleed,
The only official K-State color
Kansas State will ever need.

Purple Power Play on Poyntz Panhellenic Council

Quad

# Q

Questions, quests, and quizzes
All begin with the letter Q
To remind hard-working K-State students
Of all they have to learn and do.

Quick Cats

Reunions

Rec Complex

Royal Purple Yearbook

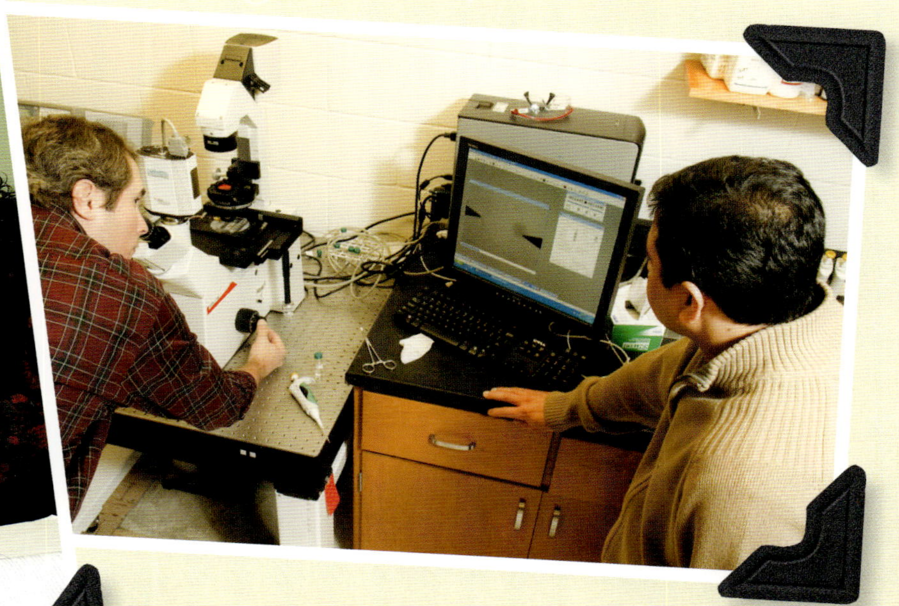

Research

# R

Riley County

Rowing

**R** stands for researchers
Who support the land grant mission,
When questions are posed and discoveries made
They toil to realize the K-State vision.

Rodeo

Registrar

ROTC

Smurthwaite Leadership Scholarship House

Summer School

Sororities

School Songs

Squirrels

Schulz

Sociology

Smith House

Salina Campus

Stacks at Hale

Study Abroad

# S

Bill Snyder Family Stadium
Proudly salutes the letter **S**
Where traditions are born and families cheer
To celebrate team spirit and success.

# T

**T** is for tailgating outside Bill Snyder Family Stadium
Preparing for a big K-State game.
Join us for delicious hotdogs and burgers
You'll be very glad you came!

# U

**U** describes our K-State Student Union
Designated as the campus place to meet.
Inside or outside at Bosco Plaza,
Relax and grab a bite to eat.

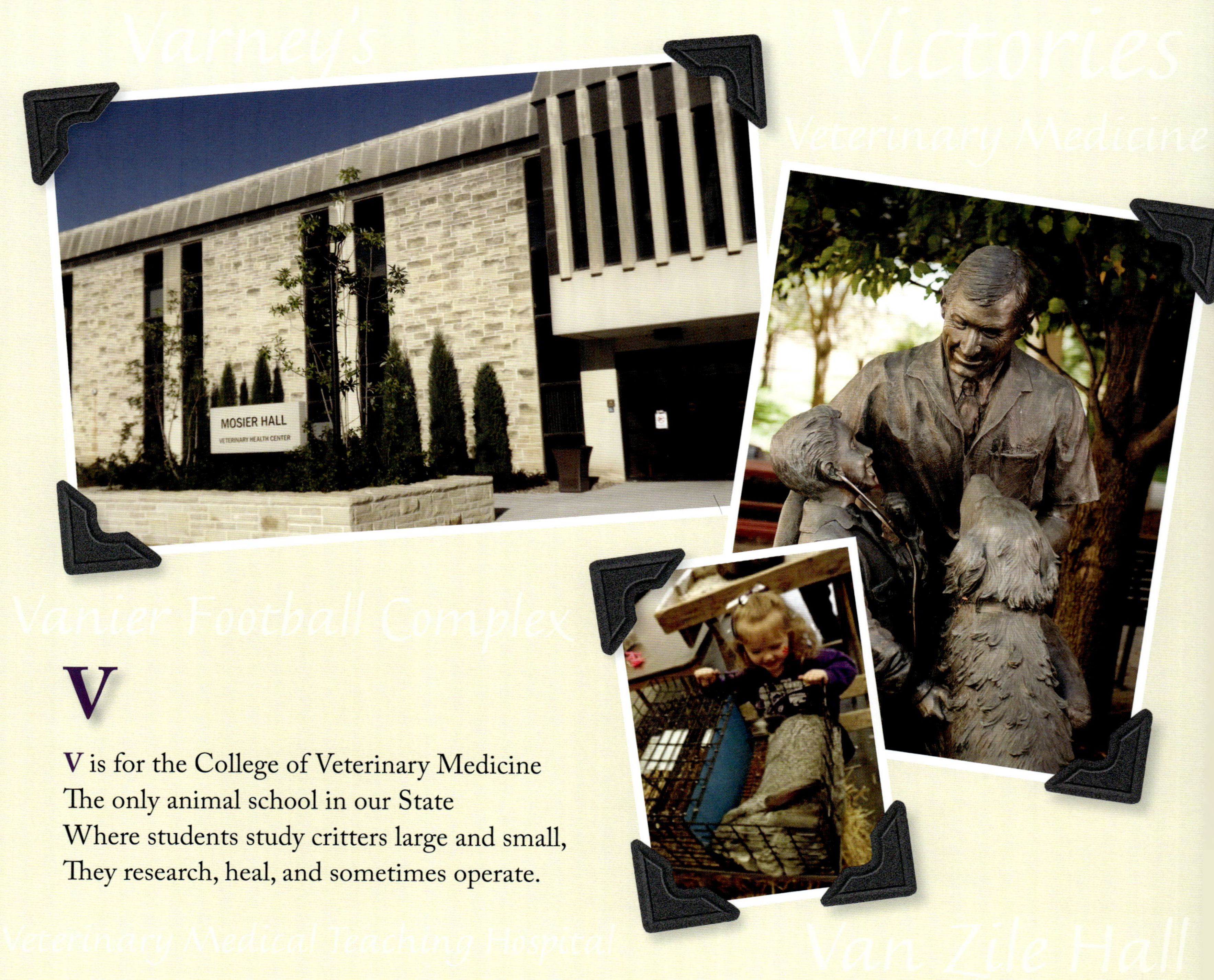


# V

**V** is for the College of Veterinary Medicine
The only animal school in our State
Where students study critters large and small,
They research, heal, and sometimes operate.

# W

**W** stands for Wagner Field
Where the Pride of Wildcat Land
Plays and rocks to the Wabash Cannonball.
We love our marching band!

Big 12

# X

Big 12 (XII) is the name of our conference
Programs and athletic teams with a common vision
As universities across the region
Unite for rivalry and competition.

XII

Yippee! We love KSU!

Yelling at the games

Yell Leaders

Young Alumni

You

# Y

**Y** displays the K-State yearbook
Royal Purple is the distinguished name
Collecting and displaying the special memories
From classes, events, and every game.

Yearbook

Years in Existence

Zeal

Zenith

# Z

Sunset Zoo

**Z** represents the zenith of life thus far,
As students successfully depart from K-State
Each graduate begins an impactful career
Thanks to the learning inside these gates.

Insect Zoo

Z Lot

Zoological Management

# Kansas State University Songs

## KSU Alma Mater

I know a spot that I love full well.
Tis not in forest nor yet in dell.
Ever it holds me with magic spell
I think of thee, Alma Mater.

K-S-U, we'll carry thy banner high,
K-S-U, long long may thy colors fly,
Loyal to thee thy children will swell the cry,
Hail, Hail, Hail, Alma Mater.

*– H.W. Jones*

## Wildcat Victory

Fight, you K-State Wildcats.
For Alma Mater Fight-Fight-Fight!
Glory in the combat for the purple and the white.
Faithful to our colors,
We shall ever be,
Fighting ever fighting for a Wildcat Victory.
GO STATE!!

*– Harry E. Erickson*

# K-State Presidents

**Joseph Denison**
1863–1873

**John Anderson**
1873–1879

**George Fairchild**
1879–1897

**Thomas Will**
1897–1899

**Ernest Nichols**
1899–1909

**Henry Waters**
1909–1917

**William Jardine**
1918–1925

**Francis Farrell**
1925–1943

**Milton Eisenhower**
1943–1950

**James McCain**
1950–1975

**Duane Acker**
1975–1986

**Jon Wefald**
1986–2009

**Kirk Schulz**
2009–

# Kansas State University Buildings

Ackert Hall
Ahearn Field House
Ahearn Gymnasium
Ahearn Natatorium
Anderson Hall
Danforth & All Faiths Chapel
Alumni Center
Beach Art Museum
Bluemont Hall
Botanical Gardens and Conservatory
Boyd Hall
Bramlage Coliseum
Brandeberry Indoor Complex
Burt Hall
Bushnell Hall Annex
Call Hall
Calvin Hall
Campus Creek Complex
Cardwell Hall
Chalmers Hall
Chemistry & Biochemistry Building
Chandler Institute for Child and Family Studies
College Court
Davenport Hall
Derby Dining Center
Dickens Hall
Dole Hall
Durland Hall

Dykstra Hall
East Stadium
Eisenhower Hall
English/Counseling Services
Fairchild Hall
Feed Technology
Fiedler Hall
Ford Hall
Goodnow Hall
Hale Library
Haymaker Hall
Holton Hall
Holtz Hall
International Student Center
Jardine Terrace Complex
Justin Hall
Kedzie Hall
King Hall
K-State Student Union
Leadership Studies Building
Leasure Hall
Marlatt Hall
McCain Auditorium
Memorial Stadium
Military Science Hall
Moore Hall
Nichols Hall
Pittman Hall
Peters Recreation Complex

President's Residence
Putnam Hall
Rathbone Hall
Seaton Hall
Shellenberger Hall
Straube House
Thompson Hall
Throckmorton Hall
Tointon Family Stadium
Umberger Hall
Van Zile Hall
Vanier Sports Complex
Veterinary Medicine Complex
Ward Hall
Waters Hall
Weber Hall
West Hall
West Stadium
Willard Hall
Wind Erosion Lab

Strong Complex
— Boyd, Putnam, Van Zile —

Kramer Complex
— Goodnow, Marlatt —

Derby Complex
— Ford, Haymaker, Moore, West —

Scan this QR code with your smartphone to take you to our Facebook page.

## We invite you to visit our Facebook page!

K-Staters everywhere are invited to tell about their journey across campus as well as beyond the University gates. Stop by and share a K-State memory!

**http://www.facebook.com/kstatealphabetbook**

All author profits from the sale of this book will benefit K-State students preparing to be educators in the College of Education.

We thank you for your support!